Biggest, Baddest Books

Biggest, Baddest Book of

GHOSTS

AARON DEYOE

Consulting Editor, Diane Craig, M.A./Reading Specialist

Super Sandcastle

An Imprint of Abdo Publishing
www.abdopublishing.com

www.abdopublishing.com

Published by Abdo Publishing, a division of ABDO, PO Box 398166, Minneapolis,
Minnesota 55439. Copyright © 2015 by Abdo Consulting Group, Inc. International
copyrights reserved in all countries. No part of this book may be reproduced in
any form without written permission from the publisher. Super SandCastle™ is a
trademark and logo of Abdo Publishing.

Printed in the United States of America, North Mankato, Minnesota
102014
012015

Editor: Liz Salzmann
Content Developer: Nancy Tuminelly
Cover and Interior Design and Production: Mighty Media, Inc.
Photo Credits: Shutterstock, National Register of Historic Places

Library of Congress Cataloging-in-Publication Data

DeYoe, Aaron.
 Biggest, baddest book of ghosts / Aaron DeYoe.
   pages cm. -- (Biggest, baddest books)
 ISBN 978-1-62403-516-6
1. Ghosts--Juvenile literature. 2. Haunted places--Juvenile literature. I. Title.
 BF1461.D495 2015
 133.1--dc23
                2014024009

Super SandCastle™ books are created by a team of professional educators, reading specialists, and
content developers around five essential components—phonemic awareness, phonics, vocabulary, text
comprehension, and fluency—to assist young readers as they develop reading skills and strategies and
increase their general knowledge. All books are written, reviewed, and leveled for guided reading, early
reading intervention, and Accelerated Reader® programs for use in shared, guided, and independent reading
and writing activities to support a balanced approach to literacy instruction.

CONTENTS

GHOSTS

G hosts are the spirits of dead people. Why would a person's spirit hang around?

UNFINISHED BUSINESS

Sometimes people die too soon. They didn't finish something important. Their ghosts may stay behind to finish it.

A LASTING IMPRESSION

People sometimes die in violent ways. Their spirits may stick to things. Things such as houses and dolls can be haunted.

VENGEANCE

Ghosts can be angry. They want **revenge** on whoever killed them.

SORTING SOULS

SPIRIT ORBS

Spirit orbs are balls of energy. They only appear in videos and pictures. Sometimes people think they see spirit orbs. But they are just specks of dust in the air.

APPARITIONS

Sometimes a ghost looks like a person or animal. This is an apparition. It usually looks like it did before it died. These are the most common type of ghosts.

POLTERGEISTS

Poltergeists can move or throw things. They can knock on doors. Sometimes they bite, scratch, and trip people.

SHADOW GHOSTS

Some ghosts hide in the shadows. Some people think they are **demon** spirits. Others say they are regular ghosts that are afraid.

GHOSTLY OBJECTS

Sometimes objects become apparitions. Boats that sink may become ghosts.

THE HUNT FOR GHOSTS

. . .

Ghost hunters look for ghosts.
They use special tools.

VIDEO CAMERA

Ghost hunters use video
cameras. They put cameras
in places that might be
haunted. They check the
video later for ghosts.

ELECTRONIC VOICE PHENOMENA (EVP) RECORDER

EVP recorders record sounds. They pick up sounds people can't hear. Sometimes these sounds are from ghosts.

ELECTROMAGNETIC FIELD (EMF) READER

Ghosts create strange electric fields. An EMF reader can detect them.

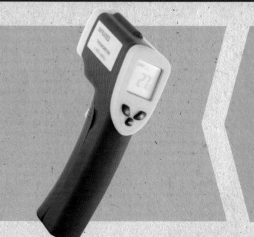

INFRARED THERMOMETER

Ghosts can change the temperature. Ghost hunters use **infrared thermometers**. They help find nearby ghosts.

Haunted Houses

THE WHALEY HOUSE

San Diego, California

The Whaley House was built in 1857. It is where Yankee Jim Robinson was hung. He was a criminal. Visitors have seen his ghost.

BLICKLING HALL

Norfolk, England

Queen Anne Boleyn lived in Blickling Hall. She was **beheaded** in 1536. People see her ghost there. She is holding her head in her lap.

MYRTLES PLANTATION

St. Francisville, Louisiana

Many ghosts live at the Myrtles Plantation. Two of them are a mother and daughter. They died of yellow fever. Their spirits are trapped in a mirror.

HOTEL CHELSEA

Many famous people have been to Hotel Chelsea. One of them was Dylan Thomas. He was a writer. He was sick while staying at the hotel. He died in a nearby hospital. People see his ghost near room 206.

THE WHITE HOUSE

Washington, D.C.

Many people see ghosts in the White House. They hear strange noises too. Some people see President Lincoln. Others see Dolley Madison.

WINCHESTER MYSTERY HOUSE

San Jose, California

Sara Winchester's husband owned the Winchester Repeating Arms Company. Sara believed that ghosts haunted her family. They were the ghosts of people killed by Winchester rifles. She built the house to please the spirits. It has stairs and doorways that go nowhere.

DOOR TO NOWHERE

FAMOUS

THE WHITE LADY

DATE: *The Middle Ages*

LOCATION: *Scotland*

There are many stories of the White Lady. They are hundreds of years old. People see her ghost where something bad happened.

AL CAPONE

DATE: *1950s*

LOCATION: *U.S.A.*

Al Capone was a criminal. He was in Alcatraz Prison. Capone liked to play the **banjo.** He practiced in the bathroom. People hear Capone's ghost playing the banjo.

GHOSTS

HEADLESS HORSEMAN

DATE: *The Middle Ages*

LOCATION: *Northern Europe*

There are many stories of a headless ghost. Sometimes the ghost warns of **death.** Sometimes he causes it.

ABRAHAM LINCOLN

DATE: *1870s*

LOCATION: *U.S.A.*

Abraham Lincoln's ghost haunts the White House. It is usually seen in the Lincoln Bedroom. That room was Lincoln's office.

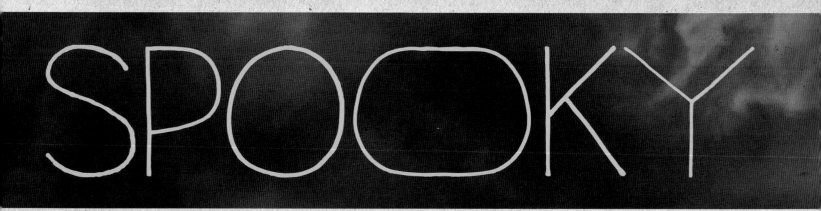

SPOOKY

PARIS CATACOMBS

A catacomb is underground. Dead bodies are kept there. There is a large catacomb in Paris. It has many rooms. The bones of six million people are there. Some of the bones are arranged in large patterns.

PLACES

GETTYSBURG BATTLEFIELD

The Battle of Gettysburg was during the Civil War. More than 7,800 soldiers died. People have seen ghosts of soldiers on the battlefield.

AOKiGaHaRa FOResT

The Aokigahara Forest is in Japan. A lot of people have died there. The forest is dark and quiet. People say the spirits of those who died stay there.

MOUNt EVEResT

Mount Everest is the tallest mountain. Many people have died climbing it. A guide says he sees ghosts on the trail. They beg for food.

BODIE, CALIFORNIA

Bodie was a gold mining town. But the gold ran out. Then Bodie became a ghost town. The spirits of the old town protect it. Anyone who steals from the town is cursed.

LOST AT SEA

THE FLYING DUTCHMAN

The Flying Dutchman is a ghost ship. Some **stories** say it was a **pirate** ship. Others base the story on a real Dutch captain. Many sailors have seen the ship.

SS Baychimo

The SS Baychimo was a **cargo** ship. It was sailing to Canada. It got stuck in ice. The crew left the ship. Later it broke free of the ice. It floated away. People have seen it sailing without a crew.

Mary Celeste

The Mary Celeste was a ship found in 1872. It was drifting in the ocean. The crew was gone. The ship's cargo was still there. The crew's personal things were there too. The crew was never found.

ARE GHOSTS REAL?

No one knows for sure. People often blame ghosts when weird things happen. Sometimes your eyes and ears can play tricks on you. Most spooky things can be easily explained. Some things remain mysteries.

WHAT DO YOU KNOW ABOUT GHOSTS?

1. SPIRIT ORBS CAN ONLY BE SEEN WITH A CAMERA. **TRUE OR FALSE?**

2. POLTERGEISTS CAN THROW THINGS. **TRUE OR FALSE?**

3. ABRAHAM LINCOLN'S GHOST IS IN GETTYSBURG. **TRUE OR FALSE?**

4. MARY CELESTE WAS THE QUEEN OF ENGLAND. **TRUE OR FALSE?**

ANSWERS: 1) TRUE 2) TRUE 3) FALSE 4) FALSE

round body, a long neck, and four or five strings.

BEHEAD – to cut off someone's head.

CARGO – goods carried on a ship, plane, or other vehicle.

DEATH – the end of life.

DEMON – an evil spirit.

INFRARED THERMOMETER – a tool used to measure the surface temperature of a person or object.

PIRATE – a person who attacks and robs ships at sea.

REVENGE – the act of hurting someone because he or she hurt you.